YEARS BEYOND THE RIVER

Also by David Axelrod

Poetry
The Open Hand
What Next, Old Knife?
The Cartographer's Melancholy
Folly
Departing by a Broken Gate
Chronicles of the Withering State
The Kingdom at Hand
Jerusalem of Grass

Sensational Nightingales: Collected Poems of Walter Pavlich
(editor)

Prose
The Eclipse I Call Father
Troubled Intimacies

YEARS BEYOND THE RIVER

David Axelrod

Terrapin Books

Terrapin Books
4 Midvale Avenue
West Caldwell, NJ 07006

www.terrapinbooks.com

ISBN: 978-1-947896-47-5
Library of Congress Control Number: 2021940591

First Edition

Cover art:
Nomad, sculpture by Trey Hill, 2018
ceramic, underglaze, powder coated steel
32" x 28" x 14"

Cover Photo: Chris Autio

Contents

IV

V

I

Balk

—before you fulfill
the performance of not being
these pasqueflowers and beargrass
radiant in the forest at dusk,

a lit face nearby
in shadows at the trailhead

saying into her phone,
the pressure to not be

in one place at the same time—
the gist of it being

lives splinter
or the waiting to admit it

is over

   —as when they called your name

and said to come inside
at the end of a spring day

to rehearse again
your sister's not being,

though by then you knew
not to obey, but linger,

listening as the contralto next door
sang lyric scales

at the open window,
enchanting and filling the garden

inside of you—
       where she falters still

in the lowest octave,
helpless as you are now

in the performance of not being
two mergansers

flying fifty-five miles an hour
along the river,

of not being hillsides
covered in balsamroot and cous

damp with melting snow,
gleaming as mottled sun departs,

the light mineral and clear.

At the Wellhead

There was going to be
a world of increase and jubilee,
prolific shade, afternoons
full of exponential ease
beside a stream and trout
skittering away like faces
erased from the final
measures of a dream.
We all waited for that,
even the dead,
who puzzled over sigils
scored into stones
someone, forgotten now,
raised at a crossroads long ago.

There was going to be
justice, the unity of one
and the infinity of June,
irrigation wheels in grain fields
singing work songs,
their casual *ch-ch-ch,*
and a silver mist
risen from the steadfast
darkness inside Earth
would drench the skift
of emergent wheat
and us, too,
the partisans of these
manifold and bumper yields.

The Music Our Son Dreamed Of

After the solstice, friable light
withdrew and scattered.
Ice fog veiled the hogbacks
and depths of field receded.

So who could say then
if a durable world or fleeting one
remained afloat
in blue ranging violet to white?

Our son heard his music's pulse
in those long twilights and soft
whir of seeds
from the crowns of firs,

in the red fox's breath
inside its lair, the muffled
thump a flying squirrel makes
landing at the mouth of its den.

He heard it resolve
into a chord as wind
sifted through pines,
then decayed to silence.

We heard it, too, at the New Year
in the way people resolved
to try and speak again
with magnitude, saying farewell

each time as if it were the last.
At dinner tonight, a child asked
would she remember the future?
The music our son dreamed of

answered the way a grouse
after taking flight
leaves the shape of itself
pressed into snow.

Apostles of Imminence

We sometimes meet people
who don't want to live
in the present.

In their darned sweaters, patched trousers,
long hair lifting in wind,

they seem startled
when we happen upon them
in the forest, bogged down
along twenty miles of drifted road.

Their wagon minus its wheels,
the woman holds the team
of sway-backed horses,

as her man repacks axle bearings
in muskrat grease.

They have grown pale
with self-reliance and want
to relitigate the past, argue history.

They are full of praise for hand-forged nails,
the striking of moveable type,
and lathing of hames.

Though for them hope went extinct,
a feathered thing, circa 1970.

And now, stranded in latter days,
they bear the melancholy burden of the past
and warn us, there is a future
only they, drilled in privation, can abide.

For the time being though,
should we help to pull them free,
they will barter with us—

goat cheese wrapped in oil cloth?
wild honeycomb?
a pint of bitters?

A Stop Along the Mullen Road

This time of year,
snow dwindles into sooty shadows,
and Earth doesn't absorb
so much as it radiates cold.

Sojourners from the mild coasts,
loiter with us a while in the chill.

Orion astride hills
in the west, bare cottonwoods
are filling with crows
reporting back from morning
forays along the valley floor.

What befell this place isn't over,
much less forgiven—
signs warn, *stay in your car,*
don't disturb the ground
beneath you, river shoals
hoard ten thousand
Troy weights of violence.

The crosses welded
to city limits signs sink
into mounds of rust.
There's our historic whorehouse,
the Jesuit's Mount of Cinders,
the eight-rope gibbet
inmates of the territorial prison
built high on the ridge.

There's the abandoned smelter
              scheduled for demolition.
    And there—tipples, timbers,
miners' graves under tailings, a plume
              creeping westward
      slow as locomotives hauling
a hundred tankers full
              of shale oil from the Dakotas
     to refineries on Indian land.

Alibis, auguries, songs
              of homeless and unmoored winters—
     we haven't much else to offer.

Hiraeth

i.

I can't tell you what word meant
to kneel in forests.

Or why people are empty-handed,
who once hauled buckets.
Where did we draw water and for whom?

I used to follow my sister
to a lake I can't find on any plat
and I forget the irregular verb
      to walk uphill carrying fresh water.

Sometimes we spilled a little under
a canopy of limbs. But I don't recall,

were there two inflections for water
spilled under barren limbs
and spilled inside a sphere of green mist?

Lives unfold the same now as then
except for our having become
transparent. Who knows

the word for fog gathering overnight
in inland valleys? Does anyone remember

ii.

the name of the clan who lived
alongside a river that sank underground?
Their festival boomed according to
an interval we couldn't forecast,
so it was always a wonder—

dancers in heavy costumes at the riverside,
drums filled with thunder,
a ritual reenactment of their route
from another river gone dry for them
elsewhere long ago.

iii.

What did we call cool and wet
if it arrived at just the right time?

What did a future do?

What time of year did we share food
in twilight, at ease with strangers
in a ring of piled stones?
The name of which remains blank.

Were those galant syllables joy
our mother sang of
when there was enough to spare?

What word did father use
whenever he pointed
to that portion of a field set aside
for reasons no one knows?

Scene with Cranes

Had my father lived, I would have learned
how to soften beeswax in my palms
and seal my ears, unswayed
by domestic accords, dullness drills—
the scent of laundered clothes
drying in light air, floorboards scrubbed
clean, the dooryard swept clear.

The July I was born, the dead already
had begun gathering in, putting by
the bounty summer unloads
into peck- and bushel-sized baskets,
cramming cellars full to the rafters
with blue-skinned squash, potatoes crated,
tiered shelves of jars stacked two high, three deep.

The time that enfolds a body's
forgetting isn't so much the time
of ripening grains, nor is it the time
a forest takes to root its own mind in place—
raptures passed along tendrils
sometimes years before reaching
climax. This autumn as last, vexed by unknowing,

miscalculation, flocks spiraling up as they form,
calling in all directions along that curve
join us. Grief hangs in cottonwoods like a skin,
woodsmoke in the air these mornings
I go out to watch pairs depart—

the number always fewer than last
I counted, but always break off

my reckonings half-finished,
           leaving the remainder odd.

Memory Hoard

i

Contrails pass above the Rockies
today, and I know my grandson
kneels up there, at a portal
in the sky, peering down
wonderstruck by this unforeseen
Earth floating beneath him, everything alive
the same age and same force
shifting through time, like water
under pressure, trying to thrust itself
through pores in granite. His father looks
over the boy's shoulder and names
the green ribbon *Columbia*,
carving itself into sere scablands.
When the river still flooded,
it remembered genealogies
of channels, oxbows, swales, and dunes,
the falls glaciers fed before dams
arrived with ditches and grains.

ii

Six months of drought and algae
still slicks the rocks below a spring.

A skink darts past—
an iridescent blue vanishing
under speckled monkeyflowers.

iii

We can follow trails north
from this valley to marshlands,
then along shores of lakes
to the burning edges
of boreal forests, arrive at tundra,
and finally stand at open sea,
ice retreating in blue leads
before our eyes, a magnitude of memory
we have no story for.

iv

I can't see farther than my friend
sitting beside me last October,
the story of her stillness and ease
filling her with amber light
and windless calm. Seeds parachuted
past us all the way down
Slick Rock Canyon. A dipper
in the creek ran underwater,
leapt onto a stone and shook dry in sun.

v

Another day, we forgot
the map someone drew for us
and didn't find our way to chanterelles.

We stumbled instead
upon Mazama ash—you can still find it
sometimes—a yellow drift below an elk wallow.

vi

Heidi, we think he said.
He'd hiked up the switchbacks

to Whatcom Pass as we rested
and watched him ascend,
unshoulder his pack
and repeat what he'd told others
about the one he loved who died
and for whom, in remembrance,
he walked. The north
and its old question posed
behind him, its silence
unfolding the reach of a year
her voice retreated deeper
into stone, irretrievable
as even the softest pulse
of any word she ever spoke.

As the Mountain Dreams It

There it is.
A glimpse of it anyway,
rising above the intervening ridge.

The dome of Glacier Peak
and headwaters of five rivers
we live alongside of

in all our feckless shambles and uproar,
Johnnies-come-lately,
ghosts of a language never learned.

At dusk, the mountain divides
shadows cast by its north-facing cirque
from alpenglow lifting along its southwest flank.

There it is. The world
as the mountain dreams it,
going on after as it went on before us—

spikes of elk sedge and calf brain
poking through duff at the edge of July snowbanks,
a whitebark pinenut splitting its seed coat

centuries later inside a nutcracker's hoard,
the fascicles unfurling five elegant seed leaves,
a little asterisk on a mountain that lost its glacier.

If people live inside some spectral order,
does it matter how
or how long we abide here?

Does whatever the mountain dreams end
without us,
if it wakes in a world we set afire?

II

Before the Fire

Thinking he could inoculate himself
against ailments of history and subsequent claims,
the pioneering hermit
carved his empty room inside a redwood.
If, through its open door, angels
came and went from that fragrant room,
however they chose and according to
purposes assigned them on Earth,
doesn't the oily film of their breath remain,
a viscid gleam like a plantain's skin
as it's uprooted? Who forgets that
stickiness, how it's invisible, in motion,
and aware of us?
Whatever substance it is,
it doesn't scrub off, however hard we try—
O, little crescents of filth under my fingernails!

Along the trail from the hermit's lodge
to the bridge across the river,
we found the words that spilled
from a child's broken bracelet—pink *divine*,
green *everlasting*, pale blue *you*—
and what better reckoning could we tender
the young, who we meant to teach
distrust of appearances? Whirling dizzily,
weren't they going to turn into butter?
Weren't their little piggies meadowlarks singing?
Wasn't a beach towel a flying cape?
And aren't we become tinder now

awaiting its arsonist and strong winds?
Aren't we the fire front, gnawing through dry scrub?
Whose oily soot coats the rail that steadies us
as we cross this bridge together?

Zone of Avoidance

All my life I've orbited with others,
everywhere invisible particles and waves
becoming a glacier that vanished,
cockleburs that snagged in wool, and that sound
a grouse's wings made just now,
feathers sieving the air as it landed under a fir.

The sky's clear enough tonight,
looking up through layers of smoke,
I can gaze backward in time from a planet
catching fire all the way along the galactic plane
twenty-six thousand light years to the center,
intervening clouds of dust obscure.

When will we begin again to foster
people like whitebark pines dwindling at treeline,
ghost forests the sphinx moth minded,
sipping from groundsel, buckwheat, penstemon—
the finitude of particular things
glowing below a spring?

All my life I've orbited with others
and haven't shifted one degree of rotation
along Orion's spiral arm,
nor, until now, just after you
brushed through flowering sage,
tasted such sweetness in the dark.

Just North of the Windy Ridge Fire

—in the lee of evening,

the candled trees rain ashes onto moss
below a spring,

monkeyflowers casting a dark hue of yellow
in scattered light.

Ten years ago, we sowed cremains here,
a grey cloud

fanning out over white sand, the freshet
carrying her

into the lake, where she sank into calmer
diffusions of blue.

Tonight, when we spark the spirit dish,
it flares and draws

agile bats who swarm from caves
in boulder fields,

who hunt in smoke that shrouds the lake,
their wings—

blood-veined and soft as a newborn's wrist—
brush our faces in the dark.

Pity Divides the Soul and Man Unmans

What do trees have to say
about the paths of disturbance
that befall forests? What agitation
going up in flames or felled by
the sawyer's chain of angry teeth?
What nuances would they praise?
How deep the soils, how moist?
How much cooler, richer
the Earth? And for how long?
Standing among friends
here in the Bitterroot foothills,
I'm as divided against myself
as these trees. It's too late
to falter at this border
where the remaining pines
who aspire to live centuries,
aren't a forest, but a crop,
a yield, a fixed, coeval stand
the value of which never surpasses
even the span of a man's life.
But if I didn't know what I was
looking at in the distance—
those charred, barren pillars
standing shoulder to shoulder
in ranks on ridges that roll away
over the horizon in the south
as though purposefully arrayed,
I might think monochromatic
fire scars blurred by distance

some kind of abstract marvel.
I always look away ashamed
whenever my eyes meet the eyes
of the madwoman my age
who beds down every night
on the concrete stoop
of our congressman's office,
and really she isn't a woman
nor am I a man anymore
than these trees are forests.

Late August in the Okanagan

In the wake of the fire front—
the stench of ashes,
skeletal pines. Teenage boys

sit inside an idling sedan
at the gas station
and can't believe their luck—

a Colville girl,
who, though she puts on a hard
brave face, cannot refuse.

She stares straight ahead
at steers and ponies,
seared obscenities

lying on their bloated sides,
dotting paddocks—
and pretends she is

merciless. We belong
to no other family
and this idea of ourselves inside

a fireproof house. Think of us
sitting here as fire sweeps through
cheatgrass, as bitterbrush

explodes, the heat turned back
by mud walls and tempered glass.
Think of this world

that caught fire, each of us crazy
to open the door
and throw ourselves into flames.

Soaking the Thirst Bag

In the end, water too
had become just
another scant standard
whereby we reckoned loss.

She led the way
across ridges, parching winds,
a rain of sparks and ash,
blackened stands of pine,
smoldering windfall.

Adrift in manias,
we brooded, old feuds
billowing ill will
and baleful mind.

How could we trust
the world soul to thirst still
for the dry bladder
and wish to soak it
all the way through?

Listen, she said
to the cold
astringent psalm
trickling across cobbles.

She pointed up the gulch,
where the north fork

once joined the south,
at a gravel bar covered
in puzzlegrass and tears
seeping from a cutbank—
the past surfacing
in the present.

She pulled me down beside her,
the air sweet with aroma
of buckbrush and mint.
We filled the thirst bag
with awe, watched it swell,

full of losses yet to be borne.

Witness Trees

i.

We've lived here long enough
to have unfolded maps
generations before us charted,
each making its claim,
albedos grown dark,
but the abiding lies
the same mare's nest
it takes lifetimes to untangle.

ii.

It started to cool at noon
and we returned along the ridge
we climbed all morning,
a glimmering sound following
close behind us on the trail,
and when we glanced back,
sleet passed through vermilion
limbs of larches and tapped
fronds of yellow bracken—
an ambient hiss and then
its soft withdrawal.

iii.

Alongside Talking Water Creek,
in a grove of joyous pines,
we renewed vows
after forty years, departed
during the Days of Awe,

and, arriving home in the valley,
smashed all our cracked
and chipped crockery with a sledge,
all the scattered shards
of insult, severings, and slander
we can't bind or undo—
and extended our hands
in offering to the trees.

Drūgath

       —our oldest word
for low water, autumn fast,
third month of famine,
drought deepening like dust
on the pack trail alongside
Bear Creek, where water
is scarcely a dream of itself
today in transit from its tarn
to the ditch that irrigated grass
when snow still fell in winter.

Down deep, sifting through
gravels, and deeper still,
seeping along fractured
seams of fault-blocks, of dikes
and rills, the oldest water,
the hydraulic memory
of rivers gone underground,
seeking for the bottom of time—

             that volume
we are only the vessels of.

October, Alone

The blue hour settles
below the north face
and lengthens into winter
months ahead, a shadow
in which half a man strays
while the other remains behind
worrying whitlow and thorn.

The stream in the forest
goes on braiding its silver plaits
over lichen-covered stones,
though the ground froze overnight
out in the open
and a lens of ice reaches from shore
toward the center of the lake.

Soft as streamside heather
under the first dusting of snow,
a voice saying it's not too late
to become this stillness and ease
inside of things steadfast,
alert to deadfall and snare,
unhindered by the dark.

The Innermost Chamber
of My Home Is Yours

Until now, I hadn't looked up all day—

it's already late October
and this month
the rains returned,

the Earth soft underfoot,
lawns in town, fescue, wildrye
and bunchgrass in the foothills,
winter wheat in the valley,

all bled together into a green film.

And for no reason at all
I glanced up the slopes
at Glass Hill, where forests
burned forty years ago

and caught a glimpse of it—
a future world
where a young aspen grove

yields back all of summer's light into air.

After Long Division

Ours, it turns out,
was neither the world
as will, nor reverie—

engines full throttle,
instinct the piston,
strife the fuel. Come

seizure of power,
our fierce bungling
warrants this

middle world
shifting toward riot
or false accord, moral zeros

shoved off the right-hand margin,
our lives just
a wire-thin spume

tides leave on littered beaches—
fractional remainders,
the grit of long division.

Attunements

Time fastened onto boxelder bugs
who gorged on leaves and seeds,
then months ago
when the weather turned cold
packed themselves tight
into crannies in the stonework.
February now, and as snow melts
and Earth thaws, a few stagger from
their refuge in the walls
empty, self-consumed.
My mother at eighty is reliving
the bewilderments of the girl she was
in wartime, newsreels in her head
unspooling aftermaths of slaughter,
the camps and piles of corpses,
Uncle Phil coming home in 1945.
Fifty years later, an owl perched on his hearth
and a garden full of hibiscus flowers,
Phil gave me a sack of seeds to sow
in my garden out west.
On the phone with her this evening,
the light grew vivid, diffused into a blue
coal sheen glowing at the windowsill.
There's no way to talk about any of this now
with my mother. I'll try to call back later.
Maybe this time we will let melting snow turn
to thought again, imagine new instruments
so finely tuned we could glean traces
of DNA from the river and summon

every living thing from oblivion into words.
The Koran I saw yesterday Shams al-Baysunghuri
illuminated in Herat centuries ago.
Every sentence the Prophet spoke
ended in a cerulean trellis full of vines,
flowers of eternity found only on Earth.

A Message Passed Between Twilights

It's years since we carried home the river cobble
from the mountain pass horse thieves
drove herds through to graze
at the headwaters of the Minam—
a cloudy violet quartz

polished by a river the cobble is
the sole evidence of, the time before
people fell into this world,
and this mountain ridge
lay at the western shore of a continent.

Climbing there again today,
we followed a set of wolf tracks
in the snow above Squaw Creek,
brooded on broken forests and what
if anything, those trees remembered of her—

whose name, what tribe, which languages,
how many Julys gathered in her,
and how long ago?—before violence
befell her and maps slurred
another woman and the place she lived.

The air so still in their battered stubs
we could guess which few
ponderosas and firs alive now
were young then, the creek resounding
in their creviced bark—the lyric

water sings even now in the cold,
splashing over every cobble in its bed
the same for us as for her. The mountain
gleamed, the sun warmed our backs
and we shared our meal in the meadow.

After so many years, that cobble
seemed to glow in its room
tonight among the orchids, a message
passed along tangled networks
branching to their thinnest mesh.

Dream of the Diplomatic Envoy

It's odd enough to find a monkey made of sticks,
or not a monkey really,
but not the revered insect either—
the walking stick—

        ambling into my dream
at the corner of Oak Street
and Linden Avenue,
uncamouflaged, uprooted refugee
from the assailed, slow-moving forests,

a fellow like me with gnarly leg-
and arm-boughs, a blunt lopped off
stub for a head, hair roots
shedding clumps of dirt, wounds
visible in his armored bark.
I welcome my arboreal guest,
just-arrived, wide-eyed,
pecker-hole ears alert, tongue—
just a tender leaf—tasting air
the way children do in summer
opening their mouths to drops of rain.

His is an original mind
at play in parks, vining up
monkeybars and brick walls,
waving halloos to the awestruck
kindergarteners passing in files,
two by two, holding hands.

I hold my friend's hand
in mine, green men who avow
the morning of the world
and covenant restored,
we're in full flower,
clouds of pollen stream from us
and I swear I'll protect
his open-to-all eagerness,
his true bonhomie,

his readiness to find comrades.

I too wish to be that forthright friend
and guide him past the wary,
past firewood gatherers,
avoiding knots of phlegmatic bullies
outside arcades, who light up
and smoke in silence, feigning disinterest in such guileless,
out of place ardor.

Given even half a chance,
they would club my friend
with the blunt end of an ax,
so loath are they to allow this
gangling, wise emissary
from the great forest councils

to deliver the dispatch entrusted to him
and that he whispered
across my pillow last night,

Brother, let there be no more diseased nature,
no ugly, no broken,
no disordered or shamed.

Mending

You knelt over the rag rug
     my grandmother wove
     from the clothes she wore—

heavy wool skirts
     and jackets she sewed
     decades ago—

it wasn't a large rug
     you mended
     with needle and thread,

but you seemed small
     at the center of it—
     those thick, colorful

braids of tartan,
     Donegal, houndstooth,
     and tweed, swirling

all around you, opening
     a portal already
     four lifetimes deep—

you laughed, looped
     another stitch, tied off
     the tailor's knot

and cut the thread with your teeth.

Salvages of Thanksgiving

The wind last night loosened all our taut lines,
lay bare cottonwoods
and this tiny refuge,
a castaway nest
hummingbirds wove from brome
and lobes of lungwort
sewn with spider's silk—

a soul hovering here still,
aware of its breath and rapid pulse,
the waking life a state of wonder
pending reprieve.

After Strife

I didn't expect this
quiet, these rows of empty
boxcars, rails and sidings
overgrown by thickets of dogwood.

At far crossings, debris fires
billow—sporadic and strange,
set ablaze by whom? And why?

In the valley, fog rimes
galleries of cottonwoods
along the river, limbs glimmering
old moon, new or full,
and once or twice each day,

whatever a day is
in this afterworld, a random wave
passes through barren
crowns of trees and dusts
the sere grass in hoar.

Peripheries only, no center holds,
a gradual blurring—

what was that, scuttling
sideways along a sagging wire,
its wings or shoulders hunched,
a lump of quills or damp fur?

A white horse takes a roll
in snow, shudders as it stands,
then disappears into a fold.

And far deeper, in the remote
and unplanted tillages,
dry thistles scrape against a plowshare
where it pulled to a halt.

The Northern Sorrow Monkey

Simia dolor borealis. *Rare across its range. Prefers highland forest near open water. Matrilineal. Not gregarious. Forms loose-knit groups only when young are present, otherwise solitary. Retreats to isolated refuges in mature trees. Browses mistletoe, clubmoss, horsetail, lungwort where available. Hemlock and red cedar provide important winter forage. Individuals observed taking salamanders and tree frogs (Grieve, 1949). Typically silent, though, when mating, copulatory vocalizations sound imitative of and sometimes are confused with the melancholy yodels and harsh howls of others with whom it shares its range.*
                    —*Field Guide to North American Monkeys*

We heard it howl from the beach below
and moments later another answered
from krumholtz high on the moonlit ridge.

The moon path led away
down the glassy lake to falls
we planned to portage days later.

Hemlocks robed in witch's beard
stood around us, attentive as we were,
startled awake and afraid of those daunted cries.

And we remembered a song, a round
first learned in kindergarten,
no, not now, not for you—probably never

for the Sorrow Monkey, too, brooding
in its dwindled sliver of life, crowded out
by refugees from a world on fire.

Nothing else is possible
beyond the already known—
there will be no adventuring forth.

Only hammering back into the familiar hole,
no achievement, no Infinite Theorem
or Hundredth Monkey, limits only.

The falls are the border never dared,
and the range of its roar cascading over cliffs,
the moonlit dome of mist,

rapids churning below—all remind how
the farther a Sorrow Monkey roves
the louder the overawing rebuke.

IV

From Late January

She dressed like a bird impersonating a man
and early this morning
perched in the fire-galled pine
near the creek. By noon, a lens of ice
spun in an eddy above the hot spring.
Steam and a thickening blue
poured through ice jams at every bend.
Not everyone we met in the mountains seemed happy,
though some people laughed
with the same affinity we felt for a raven
who'd sought out people and waited at the cabin door.

It's just a bird, the woman said, *but still*,
and the raven hopped across the threshold,
let her clean and reset its dislocated wing.
She held the raven in her lap an hour,
until the bird grew calm enough to sleep.
At twilight, we lay naked, listening
to the raven breathe
in its far corner of a snow-lit room.

Thresholds

—after Harry Martinson

Winterspring. Dusk. And the mudflat
lamentations of days drizzling at the eaves.
In garden beds, aphids cluster in leaves of kale.
Straw rots under snow. More snow, snow and rain,
then mostly just rain. The minute hand
hovering at the quarter hour.
Moss sends out velvet streamers
along the earlywood grain of cedar boards.
Hawthorn. Galls on stems of floribunda.
The pasture and its horses, backs turned
against the wind, hunkered down to wait.
Lamplight tries to shoulder aside the dusk
leaking through glass. I trim the rancid fat,
salt the discolored meat and try
in the manner of Franz Joseph Haydn
to bear this dullness of late winter—
the galant tenderness of his mind poised
at the verge of a new, more hopeful era
aspired to, but never reached.
And all this waiting latent still, high in its corner,
where wall and ceiling converge,
a pale spider upside down in its cradle of air,
an insurgent signal sweeping north,
a faint pulse throbbing inside its silk orb.

Hunger Skeleton

—for Ernest Meister

You can ski there early in April
across old snow or new,
skirt the black runoff
pooled in shallow ash sky
swales that mirror pines,
and if you ski there
into the woeful mind
of that place unfolding
its remoteness ahead of you,
your trail will one day cross
the tracks of gray wolves,
a pack hunting in parallel
hunger lines among trees,
tracks so large and many
it appalls. The indwelling part
of a soul forsakes home
and wanders between
towering columns of trauma,
the dead-animal face
that haunts and never heals.
Morning soaks into the pores
of melted ground
and far off in the forest
a flicker probes the heartwood
of a rotten snag—
its hollow drumming
the most solitary sound on Earth.

Crossing into the Deep North

The first time my sister faced the nothingness of the sea,
she pulled me close and vowed she'd swim.

And there she goes on skis into snowy pines at dusk,
this private light we learned about after internment.

Her mind is smooth with ferocity. She distrusts maps
but for all the inscrutable ones unfolding before her.

In a small town just over the border, a woman watched
my sister fret over denominations of coins

and pointed to the correct fare for two in my upturned palm.
We heard a recital on the radio that night and my sister

wondered why the pianist played a pulse of dark chords,
Is only one hand so full of grief?

In this country they say we are asleep in our outer selves,
but my sister is teaching me to jump. Be brave, she says,

I'll catch you. We've travelled as far as everyone else
with wings and the morning chorus reaches deeper north

everyday. There is my sister again, treading water
below the diving board I'm shivering at the end of.

In the blue light at the natatorium
I feel sometimes afraid, but I love my sister.

It's almost spring where we came from
and here too, we smell the ocean in the wind.

Cold Mornings of the Northern Spring

Whether you hear them or not
in the gray-lit stillness
at four a.m., there must be
finches, warblers, and sparrows
already singing, bright notes
somersaulting at the sills
of your sphagnum-lined room,
where the Apostle's boat
scuds before the wind
under bare poles, its prow
leveling into a calm bay.
This far down inside
the isolation cell of self,
you might as well be asleep
at the bottom of a cistern,
the dead recalling how
the stars appear overhead
even at noon. To wake
means departure from
one more empty station
in the diaspora of senses,
means you hazard a world
forgone, and slow recovery,
deafness having claimed
its space within you
these cold mornings
of the northern spring
when it seems you're waiting
for living sound to crescendo,

assert dominion over
this whispering voice
that always formalizes itself
into prayer, warranting
the persistent stasis of God's
failing project on Earth.

Kith & Kin

i.

It's the day my father dies
each year
for the past fifty-nine and today
for once, I hadn't thought about it—

a breeze stirred the mountainside first,
then came the strong scent of cous,
whose flower they say
smells like parsley

though it's gamier than that
and musky, a signal
that means the salmon are returning
and it's time to roast spring's first foods.

The pregnant doe glanced at us
and for once didn't flee,
but bowed her face
and went on browsing boxwood.

The younger antelope in the herd
along Booth Lane
at the middle of the valley
slowed to let the oldest lead,

stiff and thicker-bodied
than the lithe yearlings at his heels,
but still fast enough at a gallop to distance me.

A crowd gathered
at the crossroads in Cove.
A mother and her daughter
lay side by side on display in the bed
of a black Ford pickup—

two mountain lions
and the man who shot them,
retelling the hero's tale
we know so well—
only then I recalled what day it is.

   ii.
Whenever they see us now
risen from the heat of our bed,
not as Ishtar and Tammuz
but as ourselves—old and naked

and not just a little crazy with pain—
the boxelders start to dance outside of *Owl House*
and we look at them looking back at us,
wondering, what are the words for this,

what do tender engines of photosynthesis see?
The mountain lions answered
coughing up their lungs, mouths
and throats smeared with blood,

crusted with slime. Somebody is always
threatening to leave,
but doesn't,
as if to give any of it away now,
we'd have to give it all.

Summer Evenings in the
Grande Ronde Valley

Cold air tumbled down the foothills
at dusk and screech owls began
to whinny and trill in boxelders.

Roused, eyes alert, their faces
bobbed as they took in
the full measure of prey
and launched ponderous
surveys of the near dark—

that weird, agile flight
at almost
stall speed. We'd tried

to prolong the erotic
euphorias of garden and household
that sheltered us thirty years,

swerved from the open gaze
we traversed all day
and yielded
the vast room, shielding
ourselves with
hedges and shadows,
sharing our meals
in secret: wooden bowls full of August
and increase. And smaller animals?

Those careless enough to leave
their burrows and chase after
that little candle called hunger?

We recall them
in their last moments,
glancing back in wonder at
Capricorn, at
Sagittarius, at
the full moon wheeling
up above the trees—
and that yelp of surprise.

Ootheca

A year ago, sweeping out leaves
blown into the cellar, she saw the egg case
welded to a rail—the future
reposing on its cold hinge.

And walking back from the foothills today,
she found the mantis bloated,
its belly full of eggs,
staggering across the road.

Every year the forest leans closer
and each time the wind stirs
limbs rake across her bedroom windows.

When rain returns in October,
she gathers shaggy manes from the paddock
before they turn to ink.

The week her man left her here,
as during every week before it
for forty years, she harvested a teaspoon of grains
and stirred what had lived already a hundred years
into a jar of fermenting milk.

There's an emptiness in the air
these nights sallow moths graze valerian
and it's going to frost.

She laughs about the girl she was
who wanted to go on living on Earth
and never have to leave it.

Her work goes so slow now
it seldom gets done. The soreness after
thick as rusting fingers.

She carried the mantis to safety,
released it to fulfill a life's burden
in shelter under briars.

Lastness

The first word lived inside
of everything then, a buoyant
music we roused to touch
the porous surfaces of

and it's rising through us again,
gathering flecks of clay
from the bottoms of wells,
gravity drenching us in a twilit room.

Acrobatic vowels warble
across a child's tongue, answering
another child, lost to us now,
who tasted honey from that hive.

Our faces bestirred
by the old quarrels in Sheol,
we don't want to forget last things—
the station crowded everyday

with departures. Lifetimes
a thousand deep trail us,
little bits of ourselves
sloughed in rooms, farm fields,

the villages left behind,
and snowbound forests
under whose canopies we sheltered
with migrants, runaways, unmoored men.

And here we are, besotted again
at this blue hour, your hair falling red
all around us, the held and beheld
in this storm of last things.

V

After Edward Hopper

Not this room unadorned, its spare light,
nor people caught up in a story
we can't anymore deny our part in—

but this green wave of forty Aprils
since last we lived on the outwash plains
below Flathead Divide

swept us up today as we sowed fistfuls
of blue flax, fescue, and brome,
the seed whose germ—today as forty years ago—

is a future with children,
but really who can say for sure,
the skin of our dwelling in this place so thin

it's just this skift of rubble,
misremembered stories, islands in ice,
receding water, lichen, and moss,

before our granddaughter hears thunder for the first time,
throws back her head
and answers—

    let waves of color,
water and sound be a meadow in my dream,
not human aloneness, but all that watches us in wonder

streaming through wide-swung doors.

Larix Lyallii

Canker-scarred   stands of larch

    line the path   to the edge of scree

blacked by   quartz lichen

    that devours stone   grain by grain—

and these dwarf trees   here in this sliver

    of a before-world   going extinct in its own time,

alone. Oblivion,   as always

    our goal—   and today, too—

as my friends   pull away

    each into   immense, abstract spaces,

specters climbing   from one cairn

    to the next.   We pause at tree line

in the luster of summer's   depleted light,

    the north spitting   frozen rain and sleet

in our faces.   Of zero value

to anyone,   these small, pioneering,

and dauntless   flames of vermilion rise

from alpine tundra,   and grow

maybe an inch   every decade,

if they grow at all,   over five hundred years.

Song of the Memory Before Birth

When he traveled here alone
in middle-age, how roused he felt,
as though someone once carried him
up this mountain in the story of the spring
he was born. Half a lifetime later,

the first snow quelled wildfires,
and as it melted,
all the way up the draw ahead of him
syringa and honeysuckle unfolded guileless leaves
from still-smoldering ash.

Besides weariness and soot,
what traces do we expect to find
after the end of worlds—just this sticky film
in the silhouette of a sleeping child?

Each day lodges that child's plea
not to leave him so long again
with strangers.
                        We wait tonight
at the open door, blue snow
reflecting sky, cirrus casting
a golden mesh across the river bend.

Otherworld

Late afternoons this winter
traffic chased sunset
across the plateau toward the coast

and volcanoes, hunkered in a row
on the horizon, three blue abstract cones,
emerging from a cinnabar field.

The voices of Indian women
beamed from Saskatchewan
accompanied us for the last time.

Broadcasts faded to static
evangelists, the old verses
picked apart again for nuance, signs.

Even our endless disputes about the past
came to a halt in this third space—
that old soil too cold yet to seed.

How could we have known,
as we turned away, crossed the gray line
and drove north into towering night?

Those hours we spent in flight
through the dark, before passes drifted shut
and borders closed,

this grove of ponderosa—gleaming now
in late February sun, and everyone
with wings arriving daily—waited.

Years Beyond the River

i

Whenever my eyes met
a wild animal's eyes and locked—
an infinite *there*
unfolded its haven, a full stop
abstracted beyond
the gray line dividing day
from oncoming night,
each of us peering inside of,
weighing the recklessness of
the other's mind.

ii

Only that glimpse at the end
of a chain of endings—

her eyes meeting mine
in the crowd outside
the Great Synagogue
on Yom Kippur—

and no thought then
about the bereavements
of the Sixth Day, animal souls
or their absence, our names
unknown each to the other

and already erased
from the Book of Life.

iii

Her eyes were water—
the same fullness
of being as Sarah's
after the birth of Isaac,
he who laughs—the triumph

of our mother's old age
in Canaan and again
in every generation we have lived since
beyond the river.

iv

And tonight, too,
on the headland above the strait,
she gazes through me at dark ships
chained at anchor
out there in the current,
churning slowly,
the Olympics on the far shore
glowing with glacier light, and dusk
like a thin platter
hammered from golden rings,
the zenith still lit by tomorrow
dawning now over Asia.

A Lamp Left Burning

An ungainly, flightless bird,
I wander stumpland, poking at
logging debris skidders and yarders
left on the forest floor,
downy woodpeckers having loud sex

just above my head in a Douglas fir
sawyers spared
perhaps for this reason—
her stiff tail jittering
before she darts away, he pursuing.

My children, nimble as wrens, almost fly
as they dance around slash piles
that smoldered all winter
under snow, burning circles
full of grey morels.

I unfold my hawkbill—

            always this readiness
after violence recedes,
when, without warrant,
the mind resumes it reveries—

and kneel beside my sons
whose laughter makes me feel
like morning, gleaming
through thickets of young pines.

Homestead, Crooked Canyon

Hoofbeats shook the cabin on winter nights
and startled them awake.
Staring into window glass,
they saw the Arabian mare
standing out there
forty years later
in moonlight on the other side,
tossing her head,
stamping the ground.
She turned and pushed through
thickets of young pines
whose boughs shuddered and shed snow.

It took decades,
but the meadow they married in shut its eye
and the old couple stood there
alone in the forest.
Where were the friends
who sang to them—
the chorus of groomsmen,
the chorus of bridesmaids—
on their wedding day,
sitting in a circle in the shade
of a horn-crowned,
windthrown orchard?

They split wild apricots
picked that morning
and lay the halves side by side

on trays they carried into the sun to dry.
Somewhere still, those voices
laud the greatness of Earth,
the lovers, comets
and constellations,
antelope and lilies,
the hum of bees drawn to
wild fruit and pits falling
one by one into a metal pail.

That's a fainter sound today.
And the man can see
only what he feels inside
the woman, the immensity of her
embrace, the dense nervature
of the past that's woven itself
all around them now, the air
redolent with cone-laden pines—

in the beginning
as at the end of worlds—

the amber sap
warming in sunlight nearby.

Song of 47° N, 114° W

Spring's early this year
as last, the foothills already
grown white with the ardor
of syringa and wild plum,
swaths of blue lupine
and yellow balsamroot,
the Ice Age prairies
glimmering lakes again
full of camas, mule deer
turning pale as bunchgrass,
gray as wings that carried
sandhill cranes north—

our small world's here
in the middle, ready
as always, yearning
and yielding to touch.

We're Standing on the Green Line

as fine rain falls the length of Meadow Creek—

porous, scattering blue,
everything in five dimensions
dissolves into it—

sedges and bunchgrass, us, the marsh wren's song,
yellow violets and cinquefoils,
the pink hair of prairie smoke opening at our feet—

my friend's voice nearby
urges dogwoods to hold the creek bank in place—

heal the skin of the small world torn open
centuries ago, its people murdered
or driven away, returning now—

it takes that long for violence to end,
for a scent this sweet and damp to guide us
back to what's steadfast
even in its half-year absence—

the lost and dear tremble awake
like a bumblebee nest beneath our feet—

our life aboard this rotting boat
someone long ago scuttled near shore,
has grown new masts fore and aft—

its sails a green mist filled with the heat of the hive
and glimmering with the wings of bees.

Whelm

Is it even possible to forestall dispersion,
linger awhile in the air
outside our bodies, near the dew point,
become a whelm,
a gathering-in of the full aroma of June?

We never met storm-like Tom,
but when he lay down,
made a rueful joke about being
dizzy with fatigue, then didn't wake up,
we wondered—

that aromatic gust, driven ahead of rain
sweet with amber sugars of ponderosa,
balsamroot drying out, the musk
of waxy buckbrush leaves, ripening barley,
alfalfa on the morning they scythe the fields—

was *that* Tom?

        Who really can say
what Tom intended, if anything at all,
when that violent downdraft rushed along our street
and toppled the boxelder—

maybe he meant to open this room to sky,

to sun cresting the ridge
every day since, showing us this

sudden, coherent blue
and geraniums reaching for it
in a powerful upsway?

At Nine Geese Crossed the Sun

Since we last walked this ridge
with our infant son,
half a lifetime passed.
We'd just said goodbye then
to friends we didn't know
we'd never see again,
and now, wherever our line of sight ends,
we restack cairns, dust them
with rotted heartwood of fir.

Remember us, we mutter
to paintbrush, to lupine,
to exuberant ninebark and mountain foam,
to whatever language is
the light it reflects—resilience-blue,
that's our favorite, pick-the-red-and-thunder
was our son's birth color,
rush-green is milk and sun
soaked up by its cream.

We didn't live the lives we meant to either.

Acknowledgments

The author thanks the editors of the following publications in which these poems first appeared, sometimes in slightly different form or under different titles:

About Place: "Kith & Kin," "A Message Passed Between Twilights," "The Northern Sorrow Monkey"

Aji: "*Larix Layallii*," "We're Standing on the Green Line"

Bear DeLuxe: "Hunger Skeleton"

Bellingham Review: "After Long Division," "At the Wellhead," "The Innermost Chamber of My Home Is Yours"

Bracken: "After Edward Hopper"

Canary: "After Strife," "As the Mountain Dreams It," "Dream of the Diplomatic Envoy," "*Drūgath*," "Soaking the Thirst Bag"

Cascadia Review: "Cold Mornings of the Northern Spring"

Clade Song: "Attunements" (under the title "Since the Election"), "Pity Divides the Soul and Man Unmans"

Cloudbank: "*Hiraeth*," "Salvages of Thanksgiving"

The Hopper: "Apostles of Imminence," "Balk," "Summer Evenings in the Grande Ronde Valley"

Hubbub: "October, Alone"

The Meadow: "At Nine Geese Cross the Sun"

Petrichor: "Witness Trees"

saltfront: studies in human habit(at): "Zone of Avoidance"

Singing Bowl: "The Music Our Son Dreamed of"

Split Rock Review: "Scene with Cranes"

Talking River: "Ootheca" and "Years Beyond the River"

Terrain: "Just North of the Windy Ridge Fire," "Late August in the Okanogan, "Memory Hoard"

Under a Warm Green Linden: "Lastness," "Song of 47º N, 114º W"

Weber: The Contemporary West: "Before the Fire," "Homestead, Crooked Canyon," "A Stop Along the Mullen Road," "Thresholds"

"Mending" was first published in *Healing the Divide: Poems of Kindness and Connection*, ed. James Crews (Green Poets Press, 2019).

I would like to thank Jodi Varon, Christopher Howell, and James Crews for the time and care they took to read and comment on these poems. Also, I wish to thank Mary Rowland, Sandy Debano, Carrie Castleton Lowe, and Heather Swan for the walk in the rain we took together that became this book. Thank you Bruce Johnson, for all the miles we've crossed together in the Wallowas, Elkhorns and Blues. Thank you Ian Boyden, Jennifer Boyden, Nathan Lowe, Piotr Florczyk, Melissa Kwasny, Richard Kenton, and Sandy Roth for your generosity, intelligence, good will, and good company.

About the Author

David Axelrod is the author of eight previous collections of poetry, most recently *The Open Hand* (University of Washington Press, 2017). An earlier collection, *The Cartographer's Melancholy*, won the Spokane Prize and was a finalist for the Oregon Book Award. He is also the author of two collections of essays and is the editor of *basalt: a journal of fine and literary arts*. Director of the low residency MFA and Wilderness, Ecology, and Community Programs at Eastern Oregon University, he makes his home in Missoula, Montana.

www.davidaxelrod.net